# PRAISE FOR THE AUTHOR

There are three things that have always stood out with Thaddeus in my mind: (1) his optimistic attitude, (2) his never quit mindset, and (3) his ability to embrace humor and have fun, no matter what. To possess any one of these attributes is a sign that personal happiness is in store. But to possess all three is the true manifestation of God's favor.

-Juan Peasant; President at PM Group, Inc.

\*\*\*

He is a thinker, and he possesses the "IT" that most people seek. Because of his integrity, his character and reputation are never jeopardized. No way, no how. He has a lot of business objectives and visions. I've seen him progress from being single (almost miserable) to finding his Queen. His wisdom, experience, and grasp of life, family, business, and investing are unrivaled.

-Rob Wilson;
Financial Coach and Author

\*\*\*

The beautiful thing about Thad is his dedication to always being a better version of himself as a man, a husband, a father, and a friend.

-Corey Martin; Fairhope, AL Councilman Place 2

\*\*\*

Thad Garett is a pioneer among many other things. He has the will and determination to embark on new endeavors with a mindset for completing tasks. That tenacity for getting things accomplished has been a bridgebuilder for success in his life.

-Brian Adams;
Global Supplier Quality Director

# the **RELENTLESS CULTIVATION** *of you!*

## THADDEUS J. GARRETT

The Relentless Cultivation of You!

Copyright © 2021 by Thaddeus J. Garrett

Published by UpLift Them, LLC
2890 GA HWY. 212
Suite A-171 Conyers, GA 30094

www.upliftthemllc.com

ISBN for paperback: 978-0-578-97768-3

Printed in the United States of America

*"Our mouths were filled with laughter, our tongues with songs of joy. Then it was said among the nations, "The Lord has done great things for them."The Lord has done great things for us, and we are filled with joy."*

*-Psalm 126:2-3*

There is no better love than a mother's love! So, *this book is dedicated to my mother, Mrs. Inez Lee Sanders (Garrett),* a Godly, humble, and caring person who never met a stranger or created an enemy. I have never felt such unconditional love, support, and understanding, and I honor love and cherish every moment we shared.

You were full of joy, and I adored your humorous side as we enjoyed many laughs. Your greatest achievements were your children, and we truly are thankful to have had you. As a teacher, you gave all you could to your students; you loved them as your own.

Mom, you are never forgotten . . . *and your legacy is intact.*

# Table Of Content

ACKNOWLEDGMENTS .................................................................11

INTRODUCTION ......................................................................13

CHAPTER 1: WHY... THE WHO IN YOU .......................................16

CHAPTER 2: THE FAMILY CURSE OR BLESSING:

       THE CORE OF YOU .......................................................33

CHAPTER 3 ACCOUNTING FOR THE FEAR IN YOU .........................48

CHAPTER: 4 CONQUER YOUR FEAR: THE REAL YOU ......................61

MY PROMISE: THE OATH .........................................................74

CHAPTER 5: YES, YOU CAN LEAD: CLAIM THE LEADER IN YOU .........76

CHAPTER: 6 LEADERSHIP WITHIN YOU ......................................89

CHAPTER 7: TRUE FREEDOM OF THE YOU WITHIN YOU............................106

CHAPTER 8: PUT IT INTO ACTION TO FEEL GOOD ABOUT YOU .-................122

FINAL THOUGHTS ...................................................................139

LEADERSHIP AFFIIRMATIONS ....................................................141

ABOUT THE AUTHOR ..............................................................142

# ACKNOWLEDGMENTS

Family is the greatest gift one will ever have. They are the core of who you are and how you will spend your life. My promise to you is that your sacrifice will not go unnoticed nor your legacy untold. I challenge all to get to know your family history and understand your "why."

I want to acknowledge my wife, Norkesha M. Muhammad Garrett. To be a wife is to be loving, selfless, and caring; I am blessed to have you in my life. I honor, respect, and cherish you all the days of my life. You are fuel for my soul.

I profess I will provide and protect you with all I have. My love for you is endless, and I thank you for all you do. Your value is immeasurable, and it is my prayer that God continues to show us grace and mercy to age into our golden years together.

***Simply put, I love you!***

I heard once that you should sit in your mess for a period to understand why you are there. So, I am deeply grateful for all the trials and tribulations of my life that have contributed to who I've become.

To my children, Jemison and Myles Garrett, I appreciate and accept who you are . . . you are perfect the way God created you. I pray God's continued grace and mercy for you. Know that I am proud to be your father and have nothing but unconditional love for you. Success is in your DNA!

A great thank you to my family, who raised me and provided better than normal care and experiences. Their wisdom and encouragement have been a true blessing to me. As an adult, I have now realized they were some of the wisest people I know concerning all aspects of life. Indirectly, they gave me all the tools I needed to succeed in this crazy world we live in today.

I have many events, people, and situations to be thankful for throughout my life, which all hold a place in my heart, and I am genuinely grateful that God allowed me the family I have. Thank you for all you have sacrificed so that I may live the life I now live.

Thaddeus J. Garrett

# INTRODUCTION

To cultivate is "to nurture and help grow." Farmers cultivate crops, fundraising professionals cultivate donors, and celebrities cultivate their images. Ultimately, when you cultivate something, you develop it into something greater than it originally was. The Relentless Cultivation of You! is an intriguing approach and unique perspective to understanding some of the elements from our past and how they help to shape our personality, our core values, and the development, implementation, and pursuit of plans for our present and future. These elements are the road-signs or markers along the path of our journey that often establish the route we take, and this understanding gives clarity to why several people pursuing the same goal may take distinctly
different paths.

In the pages that follow, I will incorporate glimpses of my story, experiences, family makeup, and family influences both positive and negative, as well as contrast my personal strengths and weaknesses

. . . and my success and failures, with the goal of creating a connection by making the material relatable and in many cases, attainable for you.

Toward that end, the book has been presented in two distinct sections:

- Section One (chapters 1-4) addresses understanding and cultivating the uniqueness of the "who" and the "why" in each of us.

- Section Two (chapters 5-8) focuses on certain learned or acquired principles of business leadership and cultivating the leader in each of us.

While each section contains information of great value, along with opinion pieces provided by those who know me well, the content can only be transformative if you make the decision to apply it constructively and implement the lessons learned so that you can begin to nurture and develop the "you" within You!

**Let's do this!**

# WHY... THE WHO IN YOU

As a young kid growing up on the Gulf Coast of Mobile, AL, where the Azalea bushes grow wild, oak trees grow enormous, and life stands still during warm summer days, life was filled with hope, joy, and childhood adventure.

**Thaddeus, the Neighborhood Kid**
**By Robert Easter**

When I was asked to write something about Thaddeus Garrett, someone I have known my entire life, I felt honored.

Thaddeus Garrett, who I call Thad, is a true friend of mine; someone I have known ever since we were kids.

I have so many memories of this authentic friend; yes, I said authentic because he is a real friend. I'm going to share some memories Thad and I had together, not going to take up too much of your time. The most fateful moment was when we were in school; our teacher insisted that we perform some given tasks. Thad and three of us decided that we were going to put on a talent show. Back then, that day in time, break dancing was popular, so we decided that's what we wanted to do. Thad and I were on the healthy side, so picture us trying to windmill.

We didn't know if they were laughing *at us or with us*. Thad and I live around the corner from each other, so on Saturday that was our day, all the kids in the neighborhood our age used to meet up on the side of Thad's house and play some football, so when they started picking who's going to be on what team me and Thad was always the last ones to get picked, I guess you can say we weren't the better players. We could play all day on Saturday, but one thing about our parents, your butt was in church on Sunday. The summer couldn't get there fast enough; we all used to go to the Rec, which was in a park around the corner from us, where we played all kinds of games. Coming up, we didn't have everything we wanted, but we had everything needed. Our parents made sure of that. Thad has always wanted to be an entrepreneur. Every time we spoke, he always talked about opening something up; we even talked about opening a spot in downtown Mobile. He didn't stop talking about it and start putting in work. Now, look at Mr. Thaddeus Garrett! Owner of his CBD store in Georgia.

He is among the most memorable friends in my life. I still admire his personality, and I would like to meet such individuals in the future, as we need best friends to depend on in our life. Friends are chosen from the heart because of the love that we develop when we stay together. In this manner, making friends is the best experience that we can have when we are young. We should also encourage our younger ones to make friends when they are young as this helps them develop good relationships with other individuals. Up to date, we are still friends with Thad, and I hope that this relationship continues for an unforeseeable future.

\* \* \*

Most people , adult men and women can relate to their hometown as being one of the most secure places in their lives. Why is it that we rejoice and remember those times? Is it that same peace we crave as an adult person? How can we obtain that peace again? Why do we need that peace? Let's explore, and hopefully, we can gain a complete understanding of that peace we all seek.

As I look at my young son, Myles, lounging on my sofa with not a care or concern in the world, it reminds me of the security I once had with my parents. That security now is provided by God (Isaiah 47:11.) The parent child relationship, in most cases, is an unbreakable bond. Most will give their lives for their children. I would most importantly take a life to save my children, and that is the truth.

I grew up in an environment of that same security. Let's talk about the people we grew up around; this will give us a better understanding of why we are the way we are. Just a little background on me... I grew up in an extremely close family. Literally, my entire family lived on the same dead end street. We were so close that we knew the sound of the car going down the road; the wrong sound meant "lock and load." Also, I grew up responsible for the upkeep, grass cutting, and anything else someone asked of me, creating a sense of pride in my community which, as an adult, I now take pride in myself and the environment.

## Decades of Memories of The Team Captain
By Juan Peasant

Throughout the past four and a half decades, I've had a unique and special bond with Thaddeus. Our friendship began in the 3rd grade, although we had known each other a few years prior from church. Three things have always stood out with Thaddeus in my mind, (1) his optimistic attitude, (2) his never-quit mindset, and (3) his ability to embrace humor and have fun, no matter what.

As a young child, I noticed the incredibly clos knit and fun moments between him and his mother. At times, it was almost like they were brother and sister. When he and I played sports, from recreational in the parks to our football team in high school, Thaddeus was the defensive captain because of his relentless attitude to motivate and rally our squad to get focused and never give up. Throughout his career journeys, he has always been able to bring a positive attitude, no matter the work environment, because that's just who he is...

To possess any one of these attributes is a sign that personal happiness is in store. But to possess all three is the true manifestation of God's favor. I'm proud of you, my brother and friend.

# The Who of You

Ask yourself why you feel, think, or react due to the envi- ronment you grew up in . . . allow yourself to go back to a certain time. Also, this trip can open some negative doors, such as (for me) alcoholism.

Even though my life was great most of the time, I also functioned in a horrible daily occurrence of alcohol abuse by my stepfather and biological father. Alcohol was my vice. The stories I could share... but at this point not important to the place I am. We should all move forward from the negatives in our life. This environment cre- ated the desire not to become an alcoholic in my adult life; there- fore, we can turn a negative into a positive.

The "Who I am" is a man of faith by God's design. (Ephesians 2:8) I grew up among God fearing, broken people, who made us strong conquerors. This life, filled with good times and memories of Sun- day family breakfasts of liver and grits, is still considered the abso- lute best breakfast ever! Another "Who I am" moment is that I love family because of these moments. These are just a couple of things I can think of.

## Thad, the Loyal Friend

by Brian Adams

Thad Garett is a pioneer, among many other things. He has the will and determination to embark on new endeavors with a mindset for completing the tasks. That tenacity for getting things accomplished has been a bridgebuilder for success in his life. In parallel, Thad has a mind of his own and listens to opinions carefully but has enough courage to make the tough decisions.

Thad is quite passionate about family and the advancement of others. He is a very loyal friend that shows up when you need him. This attribute is quite rare In society today. Lastly, Thad is a man of God and really embraces his faith. Overall, he is a very genuine person who has found triumph in many experiences in life due to his perseverance and relentless pursuit of the visions in his life.

* * *

Now, it's your turn... who are you based on events and moments with your family growing up? Take the trip down memory lane. How do you feel? For me, it's an honor to have experienced the greatness of my family I am also thankful for the brokenness of that same family as this brokenness makes me who I am as well. Sometimes we need to sit in the hard times to understand why we were there.

Again, take some time and reflect on "why" and "who" you are, and implement this knowledge into your future. It's a powerful moment to know yourself as understanding is the key to happiness. Yes, we can be happy. It is God's promise to us.

Let me share how this makes me smile and be happy. Even though I know life will deliver hardships and awesome times; this understanding keeps me in a happy place. Nothing catches me by surprise. As you reflect on your life and account for your emotional response based on situations, are you reactive or proactive? Work towards being proactive.

Here are a few questions you can consider in order to achieve this perspective and gain insight:

- Who or what makes you feel great?
- Why does this make you feel great?
- What can you do to feel great?

Finding out your "who" begins by understanding why you move the way you move and why you respond the way you respond.

Once you understand this, then you can quickly discover who you are because if you're moving or reacting to people based on what you think they may think, then you may not understand who you really are. But if you're responding to people the way that you feel and what makes you feel great. You feel empowered. It makes you feel satisfied by the way you responded to any problem. You understand who you are. Always know your position and stand your ground.

Do not be moved by other people's opinion... instead, understand what makes you a valuable person, what makes you feel good about yourself, and what makes you a productive person. Know, this is a great feeling this makes you feel free, and freedom is a promise that God has given to all of us (Galatians 5:1). God has allowed us all freedom no one can stand in your way.

## The Why of You

Remember the "why" behind your wanting to complete that bachelor's degree, that master's degree, that PhD... Why did you spend all that time on the football field or the baseball field or the basketball court? Why are you on time to work? Why are you a member of a particular organization, fraternity, or sorority? Why do you go to the church that you attend?

These are questions you really must know the answers to and have a great understanding for why. These organizations, athletic events, or educational processes take up a lot of your time. Life is not filled with an abundant amount of time so we must use our time wisely. We must choose and understand why we engage with these activities.

Most of us have spent many years doing things under the stress of peer pressure under the stress of wanting to be accepted into certain groups or organization, and we pretty much follow the rules of these groups and organizations. We become stereotyped with those organizations. We become the people or the person that others want us to be.

Why? Why is it that most of us cannot position ourselves to be who we truly are? If you want it and you feel in your heart to be it then do so. Why is it so hard to do? Ask yourself how can you move freely? Can you move openly? Can you move without judgment? Can you move without judging? These are the questions you must answer in order to become truly aware of your why, and once you start to answer these questions you then feel a sense of freedom.

You can gain full appreciation of that organization, sporting event, church affiliation or any kind of membership that you are a part of. Please understand how you are spending your time. Know that is important to engage in a respectable, honorable, and memorable way based on your why. What is it that you need out of these events and organization? What is your goal? Understand Your goals and reasons for being a part of anything you choose. Why does it matter in your life? What benefits or sense of accomplishment will it bring to your life?

This chapter should have sparked some inner desire to understand both "who" you are and "why" you are the person you are today. Again, go back to your hometown roots, understand the environment, look at the people who were around you during your childhood, and then ask yourself some questions: who am I based on that environment and why do I have the desire to move the way that I move?

Based on what you discover, take those answers and develop a true self awareness of who you are and why you are the way you are, so that you can enjoy the freedom to live a happier life.

## REFLECTIONS

1. What does your ideal life look like?
2. What did you want to be when you were younger?
3. Who are you most inspired by? Why?
4. Who would you love to meet? What would you ask?
5. What habit would you most like to break? What habit would you most like to start?

_____

_____

_____

_____

_____

_____

_____

_____

_____

_____

# THE FAMILY CURSE
# OR BLESSING: THE CORE OF YOU

I n this chapter, we will focus on family history because we come from families with many different backgrounds, beliefs, understandings, and religious and moral codes. Families are never one dimensional. They are multi dimensional.

We can't make all people the same as each person has their own position and personality and it's up to each individual to find your position and live it the way you want. Never lose your identity! So, let's explore how your family history affects your life today:

- What about your family makes you feel a certain way?
- What about your family motivates you?
- What about your family demotivates you?
- What is it about your family that you're proud of?
- What is it about your family that you're not so proud of?

These are questions you need to ask yourself and understand about your family history so that you can progress in life in a positive way. I question anyone who tells me they have a perfect family.

Family is the one thing in life we do not get to choose. The other is death. Look into your family background and you are sure to find something of great interest. Some of the great traditions of my family are Sunday breakfast, holidays, Sunday church, family dinners, and family vacations. Also, what I thought I knew about my family as a child was not always true.

## Family Dynamics

A dynamic of some families is to keep family information away from certain people and children, such as drug abuse, homosexuality, finance, or illegal activities. These are issues that exist in all families. Now let us explore how our family history can affect our present life.

First, let us think about our present economic state. Are you comfortable? If not, just imagine if your grandparents were wealthy oil tycoons. I am sure that would change your current economic state. With that in mind, how can we change our present to impact our children's future? How do we start to build generational wealth? It is easy! Look into our family history, find the mistakes and improve... do not repeat them.

Some examples are: Did your grandparents' own property? Did they have insurance policies? Did they invest? As you can see, I never mentioned working hard because most people work hard yet die broke!

Let us focus on this matter. How is it people can work so hard and not achieve the "American Dream"? Working hard can sometimes be misleading as a lot of us grew up in households where our parents or grandparents instilled a great work ethic in us: Go out every day, punch the clock between 8 and 5, work hard, and do everything that you are told in order to receive a paycheck. At the end of the week, this was considered to be an honorable and respectful way to live life, support, and take care of your family.

## Thad, The Worker
by Derrick L. James (DJ)

If there is anyone in this world that views life with humility despite its ups and down is Thaddeus Garrett. His true spirit of perseverance comes from his family upbringing. His examples of work ethics, drive, focus, and living life started early in his life with his granddaddy as an example.

Work was never an issue with him, which has carried him through his education, business, and, most important, his family life. Thad has set many examples for those of us who have had the opportunity to meet him not just by talking it but by his actions and seeing it through.

In today's society, I found this behavior is only the means to pay bills and to keep you in a certain position of life. Yes, you need to have great work ethic and to have great moral code, but the key to financial stability is what do you own. Is it your business that you're working in? Are you working to build your own assets and values instead of building someone else's assets? Are you working from your own perspective and understanding? Are you working based on another person's perspective and understanding of wealth?

## Family Traditions and Values

When you go to work for any company, you are working for that company's benefits using that company's resources and using that company's systems. Everything you do within that company's walls is for the growth of cash flow for that company.

Ask yourself, "How I can become more in control of my financial well being? Is it by owning my own company?" Just my opinion, but not everyone is prepared to operate their own company. Some people push business ownership, but it is not an easy route. It is not what you may think. Most people think I am great at one thing but what they fail to understand is the processes of business, business strategies, and the strategic marketing planning that it takes to work your own business.

Creating your own systems and processes in rules and regulations can also be misconceived as starting your own business. I believe that there is a way to work in today's workforce world and create wealth or financial stability. How can I do that, you ask? First, how does your paycheck get dispersed? Does it go into investment accounts preferably high-interest accounts? Are you doing the proper research on money management? Are you buying precious materials such as diamonds, gold, platinum, or silver? Do you know what the core principles of wealth are?

Well, I'm not going to go into a lot of information on principles of wealth because I'm not a money manager; however, I am a researcher, so I'm going to leave that up to you to do the proper research and understand the core principles of wealth for yourself. Also, understanding how valuable it is to you and your financial stability to make purchases of precious minerals to put money into high interest savings account, as well as making sound investments.

No real advice here, just know these things will help you to improve on your financial stability. Are you a nine to five person? Do you desire to have your own business? That entrepreneurial spirit and create a business that makes money even while you are sleeping. What a feeling it is to have such a freedom of life.

So, enough about your grandparents preaching for so many years to work hard and you will achieve the "American Dream."

I would not exactly say throw that idea in the trash, but let us take that idea and enhance and build on it. Let's work hard using a moral code of conduct to create wealth for our own businesses, for our own processes, and for our own understanding in principles of managing our finances. This will give us a better success rate and better opportunities to be financially stable and to create the generational wealth that we want.

## Wealth and Traditions

One thing that I think we have lost with families of today is traditions. Remember when all members of the family would sit around the dinner table and have discussions about their day, have discussions about family problems, and solve family matters or problems sitting at that table? Remember when everyone showed up at grandmother's house for that Sunday dinner or just to sit down and have a conversation with a family elder?

These events allow for a better understanding. When better understanding leads to better execution we execute better. The result will always be positive. Showing up for the birth of a newborn baby, a birthday party, holidays, or family reunions... these things are all major events, and all had traditional value in our lives. We now live in a time where traditional values are not as important. I believe that these traditions are a direct correlation to wealth financially and emotionally. We live in a fast paced society; we want things to be quick and, in a hurry, so we are not taking the time to breathe and smell the fresh air of the life.

Embrace and enjoy the people around you and have sympathy and compassion for those people. Hear what is going on in their lives, being sympathetic and empathetic to what is going on with them and wanting the best for everybody no matter where they are. We are moving fast and always busy. Let us get back to that lifestyle where we take a minute out of our time and sit with the family.

## Cultivating Legacy for Blessings

It's a great time to build on the legacy of your family traditions; it is a great time to take those old traditions and expand upon them with new traditions and new people. Don't let the younger generation lose out on the things that made you who you are. Remember, "who" and "why" you are is based on your childhood history. So, don't let a lack of tradition within your family circle cause your

children or grandchildren to miss out on the opportunity to understand why they are the way they are because the world will teach them. I am sure you don't want that to happen.

Make a promise to yourself to take at least one family tradition that you remember and incorporate it into your family today. Explain to the younger generation why this tradition is so important and what it meant to you as a child. This will allow that tradition to become something that would go on and on and on for years to come. Your grandparents and parents will also appreciate that you took the initiative to move a tradition into the future. So, we have talked traditions based on your family history, we have talked financial stability based on your family history, now let us talk to your moral position based on your family's history. What do you believe is morally right when it comes to dealing with people? Is it okay to tell a "white lie"?

I always found this statement to be funny. What is the difference? Isn't a lie a lie? Don't be fooled... they are all just lies. Is it okay if no one is looking to do certain things simply because they do not, see? Does it mean that it did not happen? When a tree falls in the forest, does it make a sound? Yes, it does... just because you didn't see it fall doesn't mean that it didn't happen or that an impact wasn't made.

What moral code of life do you live from a moral perspective when it comes to the things that you have saw or experienced in your family history?

Ask yourself these questions:

- Do I do the right things all the time?
- Why do I not do the right thing all the time?
- Is it okay for me to deceive people?
- Is it okay for me to admit certain things in life?
- What moral code do I live by?
- Can I improve on that moral code?
- Do I live within a certain moral standard?

I found that my moral code is very sound, but that does not mean that I always do the right thing. While In college getting out into this world, I had a very good life as a young man being a football player; it opened a lot of doors, and I was able to visit a lot of universities as a five star recruit. During this time, I was exposed to many different things. Some I had never seen before in my small life living as a youngster in Mobile, Alabama. The one thing that I always tell people is that even though I made a few bad choices in my life, I always had a moral code and a position to stand on so It was easy to come back to my foundation. This foundation was given to me by my family; they always shared how to get back on track. You will fall off track in life. Understand what you have done, have a certain sense of sadness and sympathy, but move on.

When you make the wrong choices and have sympathy for the people that you've wronged, that's accountability. I was never a guy that could do wrong to other people and not have any feelings. It always made me feel bad. Even if I did not intentionally do wrong, I always felt the need to apologize. This is my moral understanding.

**What is your moral understanding?**

Now, doesn't it feel good to be able to take your family traditions, financial beliefs, and historical values and perspectives, and begin to understand your moral position? Do you need to improve on any of these things, or should they remain the same? I mean, how has it been working for you? I would venture to guess that in most cases, you should want to improve so that you can cultivate the core of you and realize the blessing that is hidden in your family history.

## REFLECTIONS

1. Think of a person you truly admire. What qualities do you like about that person?
2. How do you like to relax?
3. When was the last time you did something that you were afraid of?
4. What are you most afraid of?
5. What are you most proud of?

_____

_____

_____

_____

_____

_____

_____

_____

_____

# ACCOUNTING FOR THE
# FEAR IN YOU

Accountability is a must-have. Okay, now that you are thinking, let's attempt to bring it closer to home. Accountability: whose fault is it, and why did it happen? There go those words again. I did not get the job, the promotion, they left me, I can't . . . which by the way, needs to be excluded from your vocabulary. These are all reasons that are used when we are not accountable.

Life can sometimes beat up that five year old inside of us. Still, the real reason is always going to fall back on you because you are the one who had to do without, you are the one who did not achieve a specific goal, or you are the one who is going to suffer if a particular thing does not happen. So ultimately, you are always accountable for something that you set out to achieve. Remember Psalms 126.

Now, let us attempt to solve our accountability issues. The first order of business is to understand that Is your responsibility to establish your visions, goals, and passions. What does that mean you may ask? It means

that you are the reason for your personal success or failure. When you seek any goal or passion, you realize this is the path to a life of freedom.

## The Gladiator
by Shery Graham

When I greet Thaddeus, I always greet him by saying, "Thad, the Gladiator." As I begin to think about the characteristics of a gladiator, Thad is the epitome of a gladiator. Here's what a gladiator and Thad have in common:

1. A Gladiator/Thad always has a mission, a well thought-out plan

2. A Gladiator/Thad has a real passion for the goals he would like to achieve

3. A Gladiator/Thad pursues

4. A Gladiator/Thad takes risk. He finds there's something beyond the risk that is greater.

5. A Gladiator/Thad keeps his head in various situations he may find himself. He does not operate out of emotions but the task at hand.

6. A Gladiator/Thad knows the value of teamwork. He realizes "no man is an island," recognizes the talents of others, and knows that "team work makes the dream work." He does not receive all the glory for him self. He compliments his team and allows them to share in the victory.

7. A Gladiator/Thad is a mentor. He knows that his life experiences are not just for himself. He mentors and encourages you to find your own voice. He always pulls out the best in you.

8. A Gladiator/Thad is a strategist, adapts to change, and values and respects time.

9. A Gladiator/Thad is an alpha. He leads and is not a follower, who is unstoppable. He understands the meaning of "keep it moving."

10. A Gladiator/Thad is an intellectual who is not afraid to surround him self with great people to learn. He always studies and keeps an open mind.

I am honored to be a student of Thaddeus. I have learned so many things from our conversations about life and perseverance. Thank you for affording me the opportunity to see the progress you have made in life. You have not seen half of what's coming. Keep strategizing.

* * *

Now that we have addressed personal accountability, let's touch on relationships. Hold tight... it gets interesting. Whose fault, is it? Guess what? It is yours. The first order of business when entering a relationship with a person is to protect the heart. Well, what does that mean? It means that as a leader, your mate should be your greatest interest. Do not add undue pressure or stress. Think about how that person may always feel, live a life of selfless behavior, and understand that your reward is in God, not the person.

Accountability is one of my favorite words because accountability is something that we all must work on. It is easy for a person to say that the reason they did not is because of something or someone, or just to no account of my own.

God asked me to tell you that from now on, you are to be victorious and that you will fulfill your goals, God's promise. Your accountability is within God, and you will stop making excuses and be accountable.

# Benefits of Accountability

There is something about accountability that makes you feel all good inside when you are accountable to yourself. There is nothing anyone can take away from you; accountability makes it all better. We will have experi- ences when our accountability is going to be tested. What will you do? Will you take charge of that situation and be accountable? Would you pass it on to someone else and make excuses of why it did not happen?

Many years ago, I would not take ownership in my life when problems occurred; it was always someone else's problem, or there was a reason why I did not achieve certain goals in life. One of my biggest regrets of life is not continuing my football career. I had to be the one accountable for why my football career did not go as planned. I was the one who chose to be an alcoholic, I was the one who chose to jump off a balcony, and I was the one who chose to run with a crowd of people that were not athletes. They did not have an athlete's mindset. I was not the best I could be when it came to my football career. I am 100% responsible for my failure and missed opportunities when it comes to football. Wow! It feels good to get that all out. After coming to this understanding years later I have since been able to live a more extraordinary life. I am now a successful parent, I am a successful business owner; and I've had a career where I've been highly successful and recognized as an advertising expert. I have worked for Fortune 500 companies such as Fox NBC and CBS.

Now, can you think of a tragic event in your life that you can be accountable for, like I just did? I'll tell you what... think about it and reflect. Once you do, you will be ready to move forward at a great steady pace of life.

## Accountability Development

The development of accountability takes time. It is not something that you can learn overnight. Does it take some deep consideration in knowing why? Yes. If you did not achieve a goal and really understand why, really believing that you are the reason you did not achieve that goal — no one else, just you it's freedom to win. The truth is that if you do not achieve a goal that you set for yourself, you are the sole person that owns that failure. If you would accept the success in that goal, you also must own the failure. Now you are free to win!

Accountability development is something that every person must have, and she or he must understand in order to move forward in their life. Develop a strategy of how you would accept accountability. Let us practice. I set the goal, but did I do everything that I could to achieve it? Did I overcome obstacles that were put in my way? Realize that with any goal, there will be obstacles. Did I create the right environment? Did I surround myself with the right people? If you truly implement these strategies, you will be great. I promise.

## REFLECTIONS

1. If life stopped today, what would you regret not doing?
2. Who would you like to connect (or reconnect) with? Why?
3. What qualities do you admire in others?
4. What practical skills do you wish you had?
5. Imagine you're in your 90s. What memories would you like to have? What stories do you want to tell?

_____

_____

_____

_____

_____

_____

_____

_____

# CONQUER YOUR FEAR: THE REAL YOU

F ear is the number one killer of all productive life; it drives to not become, do, or seek new opportunities. Now, take a moment and think about how powerful that is. What does that mean to you? Some people will not even seek opportunity because they fear what may happen not what did happen, but what might happen. Always remember that you already have everything you need within you to succeed. We will never know what we can achieve until we begin to believe that we can. Fear is something every single human being has at some point in their life. Think of a time fear overcame you:

- How did you respond?
- What could you have done differently?

## A Dear Friend

by Corey Martin

This letter is to a dear friend. I have known Thad Garret for over 20+ years and still going. Over the years, as many of us, including myself, I have seen my friend's ups and downs. In those years of happiness and pain, I saw nothing but growth in those processes. The beautiful thing about Thad is his dedication to always be a better version of himself as a man, husband, father, and friend. I pray and hope my friend continues this journey to reach perfection in all categories of his life. I know that he will attain this goal because he puts God first in all his affairs. This I have seen firsthand over the years. Thank you for being a friend to my family and me. May God continue to bless you and yours. Love you, brother.

\* \* \*

When you are in dangerous, threatening, or scary situations, fear is what your body will feel. It is the ability to recognize danger and make a logical choice to either confront that fear or flee from the situation. For example, if you were to make a mistake on your job, you may hide your mistake from your boss. Although fear is handled differently by every person, it is a common emotion that everyone feels. Some seek to overcome their fears and pursue the feeling of adrenaline they get from overcoming. Others flee the situation and don't think twice about trying to overcome their fear. In worst-case scenarios, people freeze up and go into shock. I have learned to be apart of the population that seeks to overcome. There is power in overcoming.

Whether you're afraid of everything under the sun or fearless, everyone has had a fear to overcome. Fear can be a great motivator causing people to rise to the occasion and a crisis can drive them to remove themselves from a harmful situation. So, I have overcome a few in my life and believe that with determination, anyone can. I've been afraid of heights my entire life, and overcoming that fear took years. I never thought it was possible for me to be on a roller-coaster until that one day when I was in a situation that made me face my fear.

To a person without that fear, a fear of heights might seem funny, and maybe even childish. However, to a person experiencing the fear, It Is quite real and serious. I am not a person to freak out about heights anymore since I finally conquered it by getting on amusement park rides and just letting it flow.

We can learn from our fears by facing the challenges they bring. You can't just sit there and not do anything about it. Don't let time go by without facing that one challenge you have in life, which is to overcome your fear. We learn from it slowly and slowly, no matter what the outcome is. Our imagination is usually a bit too clear for our minds, and our worst-case scenarios can go above and beyond with the fears that we have for things.

In most cases, the thing we fear may not turn out as bad as we imagined. When we want to give up on something, we lack the panorama to see how things end. Maybe the most important lesson is that we do not need to remove any fear in our life; we can welcome fear into our lives and learn to cope with it. The next time you are fearful about anything, don't make it a big thing. Fight through it.

## Rational Fear

Rational fear is the fear of facing the consequences of a present situation. For example, if you know that you did not do well on an examination. The consequences are that you could not pass with flying colors. I know the fear of exams well.

Most fears can be seen as rational because there are some choices and risks you will have to take. After all, you never know if it's going to be the right choice; however, you know what you want . . . fear cannot defeat you!

## Irrational Fear

On the other hand, an irrational fear, or phobia, is an extreme, unwarranted fear linked to a specific object or event. Those afflicted by phobias understand that these reactions to specific, unthreatening stimuli are unreasonable, but are incapable of changing their behavior. As for irrational fear, it will have little probability that it may happen. For instance, you studied hard for an exam; therefore, the consequences are that you will pass with flying colors, and yet you are worried. In other words, rational fear is reality, and irrational fear is just your self-doubting mindset. Yes, we must change this behavior.

Avoiding these two fears as consistent fear, whether rational or irrational, can cause anxiety, a psychological disorder. There are some tough decisions in life some people are scared to make because any decision can be dangerous or maybe safe. I have had to make pretty difficult decisions in my life when there was a very low chance of success.

These are the kinds of decisions people are afraid of. They might overthink the worst possible thing and just lose their mind about it because fear is something we will all face for the rest of our lives. There isn't a way to avoid being scared in life unless you face it. Each choice we make is followed by our own doubts about it. These risks are planned and are considered both positive and negative consequences in life. If we carefully plan, these kinds of risks can become exciting.

If you let fear control your life, then you won't be living life to its fullest. Just because I tend to choose to face my fears head on, it's not in any way easy. We all have our fears; it can either be going on high altitudes or flying. However, when a phobia is present you may have irrational fears that may interfere with your quality of life. For example, a fear of heights may limit a person's living or employment choices. If this person is offered the job of a lifetime, however, the office is located on the very top floor, they will say no to the job due to being afraid of heights. Fear of going on an expressway can make traveling exceptionally difficult for many people with the thought of driving by it and not being in control of the situation. Most phobias are related to common everyday situations.

When a person has a phobia, they only know they are afraid of it; most people cannot explain why . . . they simply know that they fear that situation. Being afraid can quickly disrupt one's quality of life; however, facing your fears can support you in doing great things. You have a sense of being powerful, as if nothing can stop you or bring you down. When you learn to maintain yourself well in trials, you will anticipate in advance and not to be afraid. After a while, the habit will grow on you, just as it did with me, and you won't be afraid of anything because you have learned to face it.

You don't have to avoid being scared, instead, face your fears and fight them. Running away can only make your problems worse, so it is best if you toughen up and fight it. I have learned that when you overcome a problem, you gain more strength to face bigger problems later in life, but with minor issues, you can overcome them like nothing.

In the end, fear has been psychologically proven to be in our mind. Although it is an emotion that may overwhelm an individual and deter us from making critical decisions, the way we can overcome our fears is by first embracing them, so that they will not steal away our chances to grow and improve.

Fear can either become your friend or enemy. We can first begin by facing and learning from it. We should not ask ourselves whether to take risks, but which risk shall we take? Be strategic!

Do not let fear limit your earning potential! Money is the common denominator that connects all people; we all need it. We all can use more. It is used in all countries for the same purpose. Do not let fear limit your earning potential!

## REFLECTIONS

1. What is your favorite book/movie/song? Why?
2. If you could make one change in the world, what would it be?
3. What do you love to do for, or give to others (not an object. Something from you personally)?
4. What excites you?
5. What do you wish you did more of?

_____

_____

_____

_____

_____

_____

_____

_____

_____

# MY PROMISE:
# THE OATH

To destroy and defeat fear. Do not cross me, Fear, I will
conquer you. Broken Hearts, Financial bondage, Unhappiness,
Bad Marriages, Brokenness,Divorce, Death, Abuse,
Professional setbacks, Family problems,
Children . . . we fear no more.

I will stop living like I have Time! I move now. I move
with intention. I move with authority.


Thaddeus J. Garrett

# YES, YOU CAN LEAD: CLAIM THE LEADER IN YOU

What's the one thing most people desire? Drum roll... To be a leader. It's the holy grail of the common goal of all. Now, let's break down why it is the great focus of our lives. I will start by sharing that, as we have discussed and found in previous chapters, your history is the reason why you exist. Hence, here I go as a shy, young kid growing up in the great state of Alabama among a religious and spiritual family. The topic of leadership was never discussed in the home. Humility was the desired goal. The truth is you can be both.

Fortunately, I was born a leader. Even when I am not looking for leadership opportunities, they always seem to fall into my lap. My life has been based on service to others, so I regularly volunteer for committees and extend myself to help others. It is important to me to be the best leader I can; I regularly attend professional development sessions and implement my new learning into my life, both business and personal. During professional team planning meetings, I usually lead, with my coworkers looking to me for guidance and interpretation of the systems and processes. I regularly make suggestions about business development strategies.

Additionally, I was a member of various professional committees. I also completed a leadership degree from The University of Alabama. Throughout my studies, I feel I have grown as a business leader. I no longer take leadership opportunities for granted. The courses at The University of Alabama have shown me that no matter if the leadership opportunity is formal or informal, it still can have an enormous impact on success. I also attribute my leadership drive to my athletic career. I volunteered to be a youth football coach of a grade level team. The team was an incredible leadership opportunity.

I also created life lesson plans and facilitated learning opportunities for my players that aligned directly with their school curriculum and facilitated social development. If I had not participated in this youth program, I would not have taken on the additional responsibility.

My main reason for volunteering was to utilize my experiences, and I could do just that. Intuitively, I knew what worked best for my players but could never articulate why my strategies worked and why my players were so successful. My own life experiences have taught me the pedagogy behind the strategy, making it easier to explain to others.

For example, in a recent meeting, some colleagues and I were discussing business. The facilitator stated that often in the business community, there are exceptions to the rule that don't make any sense. We should just tell new business leaders that business is a crazy world.

From my point of view, I knew a better answer was that the business world was made up of many different processes, systems, and strategies that equal success. Business success is calculated 2+2=4. In the meeting, I suggested that we share this with others to help them better understand business success and why they need a calculated plan. The facilitator and the other participants were receptive to my suggestion which may end up having an impact on multiple new businesses throughout the state.

I am currently mid way on my journey of becoming an effective leader, although, I have extensive professional experience and knowledge Effective leaders, department chairs, and businesspeople are given the task of mentoring their peers. Leadership involves:

• Developing exceptional first time instructional plans.
• Modeling effective teaching strategies.
• Observing and providing constructive feedback.

Although I can say how I might accomplish these tasks with formal experience, another area of expertise is related to my leadership presence. I once failed to receive a leadership position that was perfect for my skill set. After speaking with my administrators, I realized that they didn't know much about my leadership abilities. They did not know how much I contributed to the success of my team. They did not know how much I contributed to non profits where I was a local community at risk tutoring program member. Finally, they did not know how often I mentored others, shared my expertise, created lessons, and explained teaching strategies.

In hindsight, I understand that although I positively influenced both professional colleagues and personal, my leadership presence was still relatively small. I still need to improve my ability to command attention and improve my communication skills so that others know how much I contribute to the success of all.

The first goal I have for future growth in leadership is improving my strategic thinking. As a business leader, my primary goal is the success of my business and customer satisfaction. When issues arise, my paradigm is from this perspective. However, as a leader, I (you) need to improve my ability to see the issue from a higher perspective. A perspective that takes into consideration the big picture and longer-range effects. I (you) must learn to focus on how new strategies will affect the entire population and how they will be integrated smoothly over time.

Frequently, things that affect my life also affect my comfort zone. For example, I had to pack up my entire home and move to another location. Because of my experiences in one location, I could see how my moving would positively impact my life. However, I could not help but focus on the past I would be leaving. I had to continuously remind myself that there was a bigger issue and an important reason I needed to move. Becoming more comfortable with difficult decisions, such as this, will make me become a more effective leader.

The next goal I will work towards as a leader is managing conflicts. Normally, I try to avoid conflicts. I refuse to get into heated discourse with my fellow colleagues. Learning how to handle difficult people and resolve conflicts appropriately is a necessary skill. Many times, I have witnessed people who just flat out refuse to cooperate with leadership. They have negative attitudes. Great leaders know how to take command of these adverse situations. They have an open and honest dialogue with dissenting coworkers, which requires a lot of courage and communication skills.

One quality I do possess is the ability to listen without bias. I believe that I can use this skill to help me develop those that I need to address related to conflict. The leaders that I admire the most were honest and fair. They controlled negativity through open communication. I plan to model myself after them to become the leader that I want to be.

The last goal I have for future growth is to increase my use of technology. Technology is a tool that can make an enormous impact on our lives. Teaching people how to utilize this tool to maximize learning should be the goal of all leaders. Currently, people have technology at their fingertips. Top leaders must find ways to capitalize on this aspect of our society. Currently, the use of technology in my life is solely for instruction and presentation. I would like to learn new ways to incorporate technology so that all can use it for learning.

I hope to be able to facilitate personalization, participation, interaction, and collaboration between family, friends, community partners, and the global community. Through technology, I believe those leadership strategies can transcend the four walls of my community to increase engagement and promote initiated learning.

## REFLECTIONS

1. Pretend that money is no object. What would you do?
2. What area of your life, right now, makes you feel the best? Which area makes you feel the worst? Why?
3. Let's jump forward a year. What would you like to have achieved in the past year?
4. What piece of advice would you give to five- year-old you? Sixteen-year-old you? Twenty- one-year-old you? Right now?
5. How do you want to be remembered in life?

_____

_____

_____

_____

_____

_____

_____

# LEADERSHIP WITHIN YOU

In life, we all have many relationships. Some are good and some are bad, but all can have a lasting impression on us. You must learn and take what you can from each individual relationship to understand how to progress in your future.

A Man's Man and This Girl's Friend
by Renee Alen-Alston Maisonet

Every now and then, you meet someone who you just can't figure out, at least not a first. Thad was that guy for me. When he walked into CBS Radio (V103) some years ago, he came with this high level of confidence, ruggedness, and an off beat humor. We became fast friends, often laughing and calling one another out on foolishness.

As time passed and life happened, layers were peeled back, illuminating the true person a highly aggravating, funny, kind, and sensitive guy! A loving father and husband, I call this guy friend!

# Leadership Effectiveness

There are many different approaches to leadership, which can be dependent upon the task at hand. Some leaders are authoritative, making all the decisions for group members and allowing no space for error or input. There are those who may opt to take the President Obama approach with a more democratic leadership role, inviting the ideas of others and encouraging open communication and staff participation. Then there are the servant leaders who are primarily respected and followed due to their popularity.

Although each style has its own characteristics, there is still one thing they all have in common, and that is the commitment and dedication to the betterment of an organization or cause.

## Transformational Leadership

When considering my leadership skills, I would identify myself with a more Transformational leadership style. Transformational Leadership is based on building rela- tionships and motivating staff members through a shared vision and mission. Transformational leaders typically have the charisma to communicate vision, confidence to act in a way that inspires others. They make it a point to respect all staff members. They create loyalty beyond measure. They let the team know they are important and are masters at helping people do things they weren't sure they could do by giving encouragement and praise.

As a transformational leader, I do not believe in taking the reins and ignoring the opinions of others. I believe that to truly accomplish anything major, having the input of others is very important. Motivating people to push themselves as I do and encouraging them to reach beyond their own expectations to foster confidence in themselves will only benefit the whole team in the long run and ultimately the team's goal.

Finding meaning and quality in my work is probably the most important factor contributing to my leadership skills. Some other characteristics of a transformational leader include charisma, inspiration, intellectual stimulation, and individual consideration. Transformational leaders possess self-confidence, self- direction, and an absence of internal conflict. They have insight into their followers' needs and utilize this to positively influence their followers.

Four important characteristics of the transformational leader include being an effective communicator, possessing inspirational traits, having a trustworthy character, and promoting teamwork. This leadership style is particularly effective in the workplace. Encouraging positivity and open communication allows others to feel comfortable with transformational leaders. This conveys the message to individuals that they are important and valued. The transformational leader's empathetic qualities are important when connecting with others. It enables leaders to adapt to individuals' communication styles and respect their thoughts and opinions.

The effectiveness of being a transformational leader can be seen in the workplace. They promote a healthy environment for employees and staff, which also produce improved staff satisfaction, retention, and satisfaction. This leadership style is beneficial in the workplace because it allows staff a chance to effectively communicate with their manager or leader. For example, the manager who is a transformational leader will encourage staff to voice their concerns and demonstrate patience and a certain level of respect for their opinions. The transformational manager will utilize effective communication by not responding in a sarcastic or defensive manner, leaving the door open for a better relationship with staff members.

Effectiveness of a great leader can be gauged by followers who are inspired to do work. Those leaders who take the time to gain trust and build strong relationships with others stand a greater chance of succeeding as a person in charge than those who enter with a tyrant mentality. A leader who speaks individually with each follower to determine what the follower's expectations are for the leader and future projects will give both parties a clear understanding of what to expect from each other. Having a positive and open relationship between leaders and followers allows for fewer errors and frustration from a lack of communication.

I believe that my leadership is probably one of the most desired amongst professionals. It provides structure with just the right amount of leniency to consider others' thoughts and opinions.

One of the most important realizations that can be grasped by a leader is that no one person can achieve significant outcomes alone. Behind every successful person is a team of individuals who support their leader and pave the way for success through combined efforts. A leader who makes all the decisions may be perceived as a dictator who does not value the team members' experience or ideas. Although this type of leadership displays the leader's strengths, it also exposes weaknesses that would be minimized in a team atmosphere.

Everyone must take on the leadership role at some point in their career or life, whether by choice or by force due to an emergency, so understanding one's leadership strengths and weaknesses becomes very important. As a transformational leader, I believe that I welcome constructive criticism. Successful leaders can modify their behavior to respond to their followers and circumstances while remaining true to who they are. This is critical in one's growth as a leader. Hearing how others perceive you is crucial in any leaders' ability to have loyal followers or a team in which they work.

Besides possessing amazing people skills, I believe I have integrity, an inspirational persona, motivational outlook, honesty, respect, empathy, visionary qualities, reliable, optimistic, engaging, team orientated, empowering, stable personality that will create a distinct advantage for any situation I encounter. If not the most important but one of the best qualities of a transformational leader such as myself is our ability to analyze and adjust. Do you analyze your personal life or professional life and make the proper adjustments?

This basically translates to better time management, less guess work and more time to enjoy success. Transformational leaders are particularly good at culture building, providing intellectual stimulation and individual support, modeling positive behaviors, vision-building and holding high performance expectations for all employees.

## Strengthening Weaknesses

Although not many, some weaknesses of my leadership skills are my empathy and constant need for others' input before making any major decisions, and lack of attention to detail. I believe that it is great to be empathetic, but sometimes my emotions can cloud my judgement. This can jeopardize the stability of the group and their trust in me. Also, having open communication with group members and staff does foster room for growth, but it also can hinder my confidence in my decisions. Sometimes, it is best to decide and then consult with others later about how they felt about the decision that was made.

As for my lack of attention to detail, this stems from my inability to take my eyes off the big picture. I sometimes become so focused on the result I overlook the steps needed to get there. It always helps to have some detailed orientated individuals on my team to help me identify areas that I may have overlooked.

A time where I was able to utilize my leadership skills was during my media career where I was appointed Small Business Development Manager in charge of securing new business for advertising. I was responsible for creating, analyzing, and growing small businesses and used my effective leadership skills to communicate with each business to find out what they expected from me and their expected outcome.

Before assigning each business to a plan, I asked them what special service they wanted to showcase so that I could pair them with a plan that would meet that need. This was beneficial because it not only kept the business owner thinking and interested but it also showed them that I cared about them getting the best experience possible. This leadership style was very successful as all were satisfied with how their advertising plans returned on investment. I used some of my transformational leadership skills to connect and communicate effectively.

The leadership styles that are applied by many leaders in the business setting have a direct effect on the staff's satisfaction with their job, which ultimately influences the bottom-line satisfaction of the revenues generated. Leaders dictate the vibe of their environment, so it is imperative to always be in constant communication with team members.

I believe that the transformational leadership style is the most beneficial for the business and personal setting. Transformational leaders like me inspire others to do their best, challenge themselves and achieve more than they ever imagined. To maintain the dream relationship, we must manage our business relationships.

## Accomplishing your Wildest Dreams: You, the Dreamer

For many years, jobs such as doctors, accountants, and corporate executives were considered high profile. In the last decade, careers in the field of Business have become more important due to the increasing number of prod- ucts introduced to the market and internet.

One of my many long term goals was to become a successful small business owner; this is a goal I have held near to my heart for many years. I can see myself walking into a storefront providing a product to the community that is extremely beneficial. The business grows quarter after quarter; it is a goal that I have accomplished and may change, but it is one goal that I achieved. What goals have you dreamed and achieved? Dreams are meant to be achieved!

For many teenagers, this is the leading cause of failure later in life. Many people lose their focus. I believe dreams are what life is made up of. This statement is true in the sense that if you have dreams, you have something to look forward to, something to focus on . . . even something to live for. Knowing that you are a VIP is important in the decision-making process.

To accomplish your dreams, you must first face adversity in the eye and conquer your fears. For me, the training and experience as a business developer prepared me and took time and commitment. I must constantly look at where I am now and evaluate where I need to go from here. There will never be a time in your life where you are at the top; you must keep climbing the ladder of success. Fortunately, I know that. I have a good G.P.A., I am smart. but I know there is always someone smarter than me, so I continue to expand my knowledge.

Also, there are many obstacles that will stand in my way. Most of the decisions I will make in the next ten years will have a profound impact on me as a person, as well as the society which I live. I hope that I, as a husband, father, family member, and community leader, will make good decisions because I am the future. Whether we choose to be a great leader, a drug addict, an alcoholic, or a thief. It will change the way people treat us and look at us. I know that things such as drugs will only hurt me and my future.

That is why I have made up my mind to never compromise my life or values due to peer pressure. There is only one way for me to get where I'm going, and that is through hard work and determination. I dreamed of finishing my degree from The University of Alabama, and I did.

## Dream accomplished.

The truth of the matter is that good people sometimes fail. But if they really care, they will not go down without a fight. At times, the people you think care about you most will be the ones who lead to your demise. If your friends are truly your friends, they won't make you do something you don't want to do. It is okay to say "No!" There are no problems so big you can't solve them. If you have your goals in perspective, you can accomplish them. Part of being a teenager is growing up, knowing your limits, and taking responsibility for your life. There are consequences for every action you make whether large or small. Having goals is about keeping your focus. Don't forget to see the big picture. When a situation arises, you must act not react.

It is important that you maintain a healthy lifestyle. Everyone around you is affected by the way you talk, act, and express your feelings to others. Ronald Regan once said, "If you don't have a dream, any road will get you there!" In other words, if you don't have dreams, you don't have direction.

Our professional life can be a rollercoaster ride, to say the least, so live your dreams out loud. Believe!

## REFLECTIONS

1. What makes you forget to eat and pee? In other words, what do you get so lost in that you lose track of time?
2. What can you talk about for hours that when you talk about it, you light up?
3. What did you love to do as a child?
4. If you could be remembered for 3 things after you die, what would they be?
5. If you were financially secure, what would you do with your time?

_____

_____

_____

_____

_____

_____

_____

_____

# TRUE FREEDOM OF THE YOU WITHIN YOU

E veryone wants to be free and independent from others. But what is freedom? Freedom is defined from different aspects, and according to different cultures. Freedom varies from one culture to another. Some define freedom as a natural right that human beings are born with. Freedom is the right to do what one wants, live where one wants, eat what one wants, learn what one wants, and choose the religion in which one believes, without ignoring or harming other rights.

So, how can we live free? From my point of view, we can live free by respecting others' rights to live free too. We cannot ignore the rights of people with whom we live in the society. We cannot simply do what we want and ignore others. We must take other people's rights into consideration.

The idea behind freedom is to be respectful and useful to our society. Freedom is important to everyone when one is excluded from this innate right; one will feel as if one is not a complete human being. When freedom is guaranteed, I can think freely, go where I want, say my opinion without fear from people who would not like my opinion. Freedom of opinion is among the most important branches of freedom.

In some societies where freedom of opinion is not guaranteed by the authority, the creativity of the mind is killed and buried. Society is the largest and biggest loser from this lack of creativity. Someone once said, Freedom of opinion will never result in animosity among people if they respect each other.

As I mentioned earlier, freedom is not an absolute right, and there are too many constraints on it. First, national security which is very important. Security is as important as freedom. Our practicing of freedom should never lead to threatening our security. Second, freedom of belief, to believe in what you want and choose religion. We also should have the right to establish our own places, where we perform our religious actions.

Historically, there has been proof that freedom is innate to humans and that he will fight if he lives to restore his innate right to be a free man. The western civilization guaranteed freedom for its own people and occupied poor nations and deprived their people of their rights, including freedom. So, these poor nations fought without rest to restore freedom and autonomy from occupation. Abduction of rights is not a respectful human action. Since God gave us freedom for free, we must do our best to maintain and keep this right?

Among the most humiliating ways to punish a human, is to deprive him of freedom. When one goes to jail, he is deprived of his freedom, and so he is suffering, which is the point of punishment. Lacking freedom teaches the human lessons. If he will make use of it. Freedom cannot be felt right, unless one tastes lack of freedom, then he will really appreciate freedom from his depths.

Freedom is not absolute. Freedom must be limited. You cannot just do what you like and say, "I am a free man". You cannot kill, smuggle drugs, or violate the laws and rules for freedom's sake. There should be respect to other people and their needs.

Once, there were two men  sitting side by side, and one of the men lifted his hand and touched the other's nose, and the latter complained, and the     said, "I am free?" This was as a dismay to the latter    who was ready with an appalling answer, and said, "The freedom of your hand ends where the freedom of my nose begins." Yes, the freedom of anyone ends where the freedom of another one begins.

Parents must teach their youngsters to be free. They must plant in them the love for freedom, but their freedom must indeed be watched. It should not be without limits. We must consider ways to censor their behavior without fear of being ridiculed by their friends.

Freedom in the teen years is very important for building a good character and stable personality. Teens want to hang around with friends, do whatever they like, or sometimes do not like. They want to experience everything. If they are given freedom with no limits, they can go down to the base and may be lost. So, we must watch their behavior, teach them to do what is right and leave what is wrong. Such supervision is generally not considered a limit or constraint on freedom. It is, important for the protection of existence. Freedom alone may lead to bad actions and cause destruction in the society. The most important thing that we must care about is enjoying our freedom without harming our security. In hard times, like terrorist attacks, constraints may be imposed on freedom for general protection of the existence of the community, but this is only a timed condition that shall end soon after a catastrophic condition ends.

So, freedom is an innate right that humans are born with. Nothing should threaten our freedom or deprive us from our rights. Also, our right to freedom must never harm any other human being, directly or indirectly. We must respect the freedom of everyone in the society. This way we can enjoy our freedom through our life.

## Motivational Triggers: Believe What You are telling yourself

Overall, motivation is "The general desire or willingness of someone to do something." For me, motivation plays a significant role in accomplishing goals, working harder, and being successful. Internal and external forces also have a powerful impact on my motivation. I discovered that my motivation stems from both internal and external forces equally.

Sometimes, however motivation is lacking when doing something unpleasant or undesirable, such as writing an essay. Thankfully, there are numerous ways to increase motivation. "Motivation and enthusiasm manifest as desire and interest, and as a driving force that pushes you to take action and pursue goals."

Motivation can influence behavior in multiple ways. I know for me that my behavior and decisions have been impacted by my motivation. I am very goal oriented, and I have the ambition and drive to work harder to achieve my goals. My freshman year in high school, after making the varsity football team, I decided I wanted to become a professional football player and I sharpened my skills. I knew this would be a long-term goal and I would have to give it my all if I wanted to achieve it.

Once I had this objective in mind, I became highly motivated to do well at football so that I could go to a reputable college. After realizing my goal, I worked harder in high school, held leadership positions in clubs, and even obtained a starting position to gain experience. Now looking back at high school, I understand how my motivation and determination influenced my behavior. All of this resulted from being motivated to achieve my goal to become a professional athlete.

Intrinsic motivation is "a motivation to take actions that are themselves rewarding;" as compared to extrinsic motivation which is "a motivation to take actions that are not themselves rewarding but that lead to reward". Personally, my motivation equally stems from intrinsic and extrinsic forces. I find it rewarding, even enjoyable, to work hard and learn new things, which is the main part of my intrinsic motivation. However, the rest of my motivation originates from external forces.

We have all heard the famous quote, "You learn from your mistakes," which is very true for me except I also learn from other people's mistakes as well. As the oldest of two children, I learned a great deal from my younger sister. She is three years my junior and started high school when I was a Senior. She is the total opposite of me. She was very focused on education and following the rules. Her discipline was something that I could benefit from as she was always better with money and time management. When she went to college, she finished at the top of her class. I saw the rewards of my sister's actions and from that moment I knew I could benefit from her personality and style.

My sister's actions are an external force and are one of the key reasons why I am so motivated to succeed. Now I push myself every day to be better and prioritize my responsibilities. The teachings of my sister's actions motivated me. Another way that I am externally motivated is that I do not want to disappoint others. Sometimes, I feel that I will disappoint others if I fail. These are the main reasons why I am motivated to work so hard to accomplish my goals. I want to be successful and avoid negative outcomes that would be disappointing to others.

Since I enjoy studying (internal force), and I have learned from my sister's behavior (external force), both of these forces have increased my motivation and drive to be successful.

Motivation is necessary to achieve a desired goal. Motivation is even more vital to complete a task that we would not usually be motivated to do. Thankfully, multiple techniques can be used to increase motivation. It happens quite often that we are required to complete a task that might be difficult or tedious and we have little motivation to complete it. This leads to procrastination and a mediocre completion of the task. Thinking about the benefits of doing the task and the consequences of not completing the task, is a great way to increase motivation. Usually by thinking how the task can be beneficial, one will feel more satisfied when the task is completed. On the other hand, by considering the consequences of not completing the task can help motivate one to complete it. Studying for a test, for example, might not always be enjoyable, but thinking about how pleasant it is to earn a good grade on the test could motivate one to study. Also, thinking of the consequences of receiving a low grade on the test from not studying, could motivate one to study to avoid that outcome. Both techniques are effective ways to increase motivation. Similarly, breaking down tasks into simple steps is another way to increase motivation.

Another way to increase motivation to complete a task that might not be fun, or desirable is to divide the task into smaller and more accomplishable steps. It is easy to become overwhelmed completing a task that one might not enjoy. Breaking down the task into smaller steps can relieve some of the anxiety of completing it.

An example of this for me would be writing a research paper. Personally, writing a research paper can be challenging and overwhelming, especially if I wait until the last minute. To ease the process of writing a research paper, I break the paper down into multiple steps. I start by gathering information and resources and then come up with an outline.

Next, I begin coming up with ideas for the topic and how I will organize my paper and write the rough draft. Finally, I edit the paper and prepare to publish. This way relieves some of the stress of trying to write the paper all at once.

Once I start a task and see progress, it becomes easier to accomplish it.

# Implementing the Art of Motivation

Overall, if we are not motivated, we would never accomplish anything. Motivation provides us with the drive and ambition necessary to complete goals. Motivation has greatly impacted my behavior and increased my initiative to work harder to accomplish my objectives.

Once again, I find that both internal and external forces contribute to my motivation equally. Both these forces combined have increased my desire to succeed. While we might find it hard to find motivation to complete undesirable tasks, there are numerous ways to increase motivation.

Sometimes in life there is no reward in finishing a task, but these tasks have to be completed, regardless of our motivation, because that is just life. In general, motivation plays a powerful role in our ability to accomplish anything.

What drives you? If you don't know the answer to this question, you're not living to your full potential. *So, let's get motivated.*

## REFLECTIONS

1. What is working well for you in your current life & career? What do you find fulfilling, meaningful, enjoyable, and important?
2. What isn't working for you? What drains you, makes you stressed, or wastes your time?
3. What role has formal education played in your life and how do you feel about it?
4. Do you believe your destiny is pre-determined or in your hands to shape however you wish?
5. What do you believe is the meaning of your life?

_____

_____

_____

_____

_____

_____

# PUT IT INTO ACTION
# TO FEEL GOOD ABOUT YOU

There have been many great leaders down through history. Leaders who have influenced change throughout many aspects of society.

Great leaders have great influence. The effectiveness of a leader is determined by his leadership style. With so many styles to choose from, and the fact that not one style fits all situations, becoming an effective leader is a challenging task. One reflective note is that it is important to cultivate good leadership skills. One must evaluate personal strengths and weaknesses and consider making changes as the situation demands a different leadership style.

An assessment of an individual's strengths and weaknesses makes it possible for the individual to grow in skill and knowledge. Throughout the assessment experience it became apparent that, although I have extensive experience in leadership within business development, I lack knowledge and experience in leadership roles in the entrepreneurial world.

Through the assessment process, I discovered that I consider the person to be as important as the task. People need to be nurtured and encouraged; they need to trust their leader to be knowledgeable and skilled. When given a task, people need to be empowered to accomplish it. Just as students need to learn it is necessary for me to be a life-long learner.

## Thad The Thinker
by Rob Wilson

Thad and I have been friends for almost a decade, having met at CBS Radio. We shared a common friend with whom we shared many sporting events, travels, and other activities. During that time, I learned a great deal about him. When we first met, he was a single father, and his bond with his son, Myles, was fascinating to watch. With "roll tide," he has serious biases.

He is a thinker, and he possesses the "IT" that most people seek. Because of his integrity, his character and reputation are never jeopardized. No way, no how. He has a lot of business objectives and visions. I've seen him progress from being single (almost miserable) to finding his Queen. His wisdom, experience, and grasp of life, family, business, and investing are unrivaled.

I am grateful for the opportunity to tell him about the kind of man he is while he is still with us. I would fight with him in a foxhole — not to cover his back but knowing he'll be covering mine. Grateful for you...

## Types of Leadership

When studying the various types of leadership one can become overwhelmed. There are four types of leadership that stood out in my studies. The four types are:

1. Situational Theory
2. Visionary Leadership
3. Blake-Mouton Managerial Grid
4. Transformational Leadership

Each of these styles show varying ways to lead that I have seen exemplified in the lives of leaders through history. The Situational theory proposes that leaders choose the best course of action based upon situational variables. Different styles of leadership may be more appropriate for certain types of decision-making, the situation called for a different type of leadership than presented.

## Visionary Leadership

When considering leadership, it would be difficult to overlook the most prominent of any group of Founding Fathers, George Washington. George Washington was a visionary leader.

A visionary leader has a vision that he can instill in others. He creates a culture in which people believe in and value his vision making it possible to attain his goals. George Washington had a vision to win the war, no matter how long it took. Second, he had a vision of independence from Great Britain. He looked to the future and saw a republic with a constitutional government, a government of elected individuals leading this country.

Being a visionary leader, he would stay the course and the representatives that elected him saw this in him. This vision is what got him elected as General and Commander in Chief of the United Colonies.

## Blake-Mouton Managerial Grid

The Blake-Mouton Managerial Grid was developed in 1964. This original model identified five different lead- ership styles:

- Authority-Compliance: This style is very authoritative. The
  leader has all the power and makes all the decisions.
- Country Club Management: In this management style, the
  leader places importance on the feelings of the people. This is
  an informal managment system. Everyone is working together.

- Impoverished Management: This style displays a management style in which the leader is uninvolved.

- Middle-of-the-Road Management: This management style exemplifies compromise. A task is presented with why it should be completed, and everyone is expected to fall in line.

- Team Management: This style employs teamwork, cooperation, participation, and commitment to reach their goals. Communication between leader and subordinates leads to fewer misunderstandings and there is a stronger sense of self-control rather than control over individuals.

## Transformational Leadership

The transformational leader desires to transform the organization. This transformation comes about because of the connection the leader has with his followers. The trans- formational leader provides the team with a vision. The enthusiasm and energy of the leader inspires the followers to fulfill that vision. It is believed and espoused by the transformational leader that change takes place not only in the fulfilling of the vision but also in the followers.

## Leadership Skills

With all this knowledge of leadership one must put it into practice. To do this a framework of twelve skills have been developed. These twelve leadership skills are:

1. Developing trusting relationships
2. Leading in the realization of the vision
3. Making quality decisions
4. Communicating effectively
5. Resolving conflict and issues
6. Motivating and developing others
7. Managing group processes
8. Supporting others with appropriate leadership style
9. Using power ethically
10. Creating and managing a positive culture and climate
11. Initiating change
12. Evaluating personnel and performance

Within this framework a leader can reflect on the application of the skills practiced determining the need for further development to improve the organization. The primary skill would be to build and develop trust. It is the foundation to the other skills. If the leader is not trusted by his subordinates, then change will be difficult, conflicts arise, people are not motivated to perform, and the culture and climate of the work environment is not positive. People will not be loyal to the leader and will seek employment somewhere else.

## Leadership Approach

To determine my approach to leadership I must define leadership. To be a leader a person must be able to moti- vate others, encourage personal growth and development of skills, develop trust, be a lifelong learner, have a passion for their vision, and personal concern for one's followers. In over 25 years of business leadership, I have had several good leaders. My first was my third-grade teacher, Mrs. Patterson, who placed me in a reading group of strong readers in midyear. She came by regularly to monitor the progress of my reading out loud and comfort with other students, especially since I didn't read very well. I was one of four weaker readers in the class. Mrs. Patterson gave me the resources and encouragement that I needed to help me be successful. Several years later I was confident and reading in front of large crowds.

The next was a manager he utilized collaboration among the team to build relationships. Because he built relationships, people were focused on performance. We all worked hard, attended workshops, challenged ourselves, and communicated expectations with one another. I really enjoyed collaborating with my colleagues so that I could reach my goals and be prepared for the challenges.

Currently, my wife, Norkesha, is a manager. More importantly she is my manager. The completion of tasks is very important to her. The sooner you get it done, the better off you are with her. She always has a list. I can see that being organized is very important to her.

Having walked in the shadow of several leaders, I feel that I will draw the best from them. Building trust and relationships will be important to me. I continually assess my skills as a leader and seek to improve myself through readings and conferences.

Reading leadership articles frequently has broadened my views of leadership. Reflecting on the different theories and styles has caused me to think about how I currently lead within my home, my business, and among my friends. I believe that I will lead according to the situation. I am more aware of the different approaches available, for example, autocratic and democratic. I know that not one style fits all situations. I am also more aware of my temperament, Guardian, playing a role in my actions and decisions.

Becoming an effective leader is the goal that is set before me. After the readings of this book and research of other sources it seems to be a challenging task. However, many have accomplished this task before me. With the encouragement of my family, friends, and colleagues, because they see in me the potential to be a leader that makes a difference, I can do this and so can you.

## A Tale of Two Thaddeuses

by Franz Lynch

My experiences with Thaddeus Garret started at least nine or ten years ago when he came to work at CBS Radio in Atlanta. Thaddeus had a digital background, which was in high demand in the radio business as we pivoted to digital audio and social media. As with most digital recruits, Thaddeus did not stay long as our "radio digital" was very different from what the recruits were accustomed to in their previous positions.

Despite his departure from CBS, our relationship grew over the years. Thad became one of my best friends. We spent a good deal of time together. When I met Thad, he was married and had a baby boy named Myles. Tha did not drink to my knowledge, and he was pretty much committed to the house-husband scene. It was not until after his divorce that our friendship really took off. Thad and I, along with another good friend of ours, spent a lot of our time at sports bars or cigar lounges. Both Thad and I were single and enjoyed striking up conversations with women we would meet when we were out.

I had noticed that the rather reserved Thaddeus I had met when he was married was not as mild-mannered and considerate to some of the women we encountered when we were enjoying our single status. It appeared his experiences from his divorce had changed him in a way that was not becoming.

We would talk about it, and he confirmed that he was a different person as a single man and wished to find his next partner and be in a committed relationship. He recognized that he was, in fact, a better person when in a relationship. I watched him search for his "rib," so to speak, and I could see he was more serious about his selection than when he first got divorced. He was not looking to just date and move on, but he was looking for his life partners.

Not too long after, he met his now-wife, Kesha, and moved quickly to take it to the next level. I was concerned that he had not spent much time with her to move so fast, but he was certain that she was it. In what seemed like months, Thad was engaged... and then married. What I witnessed next was nothing short of a metamorphosis. Thaddeus and Kesha's relationship had produced a transformation that Thad had predicted. His love and commitment to her went beyond their relationship but deep into his personal and professional growth.

Today, they are a model couple — working together to create a better life for not only themselves but others around them. I don't believe that Kesha changed him, however. I believe that she helped him take the focus off himself and his fears and failures, allowing him to focus on his true nature. I'm sure it's easier to overcome our fears when we have a committed partner at our side.

## REFLECTIONS

1. Who is a person that you don't like yet you spend time with?
2. What is something that is true for you no matter what?
3. What is your moral compass in making difficult decisions?
4. What is one failure that you have turned into your greatest lesson?
5. What role does gratitude play in your life?

_____

_____

_____

_____

_____

_____

_____

_____

_____

# FINAL THOUGHTS

I spent many years of my life living the so called dream. Little did I know it was not my dream but the dream of other people. There is a statement that "You can't see the forest for the trees." I have lived that statement to the max, and I know I am not the only one. We are supposed to live our lives based on our own principles, morals, and expectations, but not many of us do. How many of us are trapped in the box of what others think, live, or do?

Today, I have gained a freedom that is like no other feeling I have ever had. I realized if I was going to grow, I must live out my dream and become who I want to be with no regrets or apologies. After becoming woke, I have been a student in spiritual development; I am confident in God's promise, and I cannot be moved. My faith has been renewed to an all time high, and I have witnessed the manifestations of God when I thought there was no way possible. I've watched the impossible become "the normal" in my life all because I made a choice to live my dream.

You might be thinking, what is my dream? Is it only to live outside the box of broken hearts, financial bondage, unhappiness, bad marriage, brokenness, divorce, death, and abuse?

Living your freedom enables you to discover your true purpose in life. One where you can not only accomplish your goals, but you can also live a life that will generate a legacy for your children. When you improve our life, there is a positive effect on all the people around you, and that is the way you build a better world.

It is my hope that the lessons I have shared in this book will help to improve your perspective on life and have a positive impact on you for decades to come. Let my journey be the bridge you don't have to build and encourage you to relentlessly cultivate the YOU within You!

# LEADERSHIP
# AFFIIRMATIONS

Time to shine and grind. Failure is always the win.
By attempting to control the outcome, you miss the moment.

Stop living like you have time!

Knowledge without implementation is unacceptable.

Conquer the dream within you!

But did you die?!

# ABOUT THE AUTHOR

Thaddeus J. Garrett is a man of unbreakable faith, a devoted husband, committed father, and unconditional family man. Also, just a simple man who follows his passions and loves the beach. He believes you have all you need inside to live your wildest dreams, so why not?

His hometown is Mobile, Alabama, the absolute best place to grow up. He became a 5-star athlete recruited by Division 1 SEC colleges in 1992 and significantly place where he began his leadership journey. But now, he resides in Atlanta, GA. He is a graduate of the University of Mobile, where he studied business; his most accomplished degree was obtained from The University of Alabama. He majored in Interdisciplinary Leadership, conquering a desire that existed since 1992.

*He made a promise and kept it!*

Thaddeus has a vast amount of experience in exceeding business goals, personal goals, leadership goals, and community service goals. His past professional experiences include many years with major broadcast communication powerhouses such as FOX, UPN, NBC, and CBS. He worked his way from the bottom to an executive role.

In 2003, he created "The AM Group," the first full- service digital ad agency

Made in the USA
Columbia, SC
24 October 2021